Maths at Work

Maths on the Farm

Tracey Steffora

Raintree

Raintree is an imprint of Capstone Global Library Limited, a company incorporated in England and Wales having its registered office at 7 Pilgrim Street, London, EC4V 6LB – Registered company number: 6695582

www.raintreepublishers.co.uk
myorders@raintreepublishers.co.uk

Text © Capstone Global Library Limited 2013
First published in hardback in 2013
Paperback edition first published in 2014
The moral rights of the proprietor have been asserted.

Edited by Dan Nunn and Abby Colich
Designed by Victoria Allen
Picture research by Tracy Cummins
Production control by Victoria Fitzgerald
Printed and bound in China by Leo Paper Products Ltd

ISBN 978 1 406 25076 3 (hardback)
16 15 14 13 12
10 9 8 7 6 5 4 3 2 1

ISBN 978 1 406 25083 1 (paperback)
17 16 15 14 13
10 9 8 7 6 5 4 3 2 1

British Library Cataloguing in Publication Data
Steffora, Tracey.
Maths on the farm. – (Maths at work)
510-dc23
A full catalogue record for this book is available from the British Library.

Acknowledgements
We would like to thank the following for permission to reproduce photographs: Corbis: pp. 8 (© Ian Lishman/ Juice Images), 12 (© Juice Images); Getty Images: pp. 10 (Cultura/Monty Rakusen), 11 (Simon Rawles), 14 (Dr. Marli Miller); iStockphoto: pp. 7 (© Dan Moore), 19 (© emholk), 21 (© Gord Horne), 23a (© Gord Horne); Shutterstock: pp. 4 (Noam Armonn), 5 (Goodluz), 6 (Denis and Yulia Pogostins), 9 (Burry van den Brink), 13 (picsbyst), 15 (Vladislav Gajic), 16 (Gemenacom), 17 (Deymos), 20 (Denis and Yulia Pogostins), 23b (Denis and Yulia Pogostins); Superstock: p. 18 (© imagebroker.net).

Front cover photograph of a man feeding chickens outdoors reproduced with permission from Getty Images (Johnny Valley).

Back cover photograph of a hand holding seeds reproduced with permission from Shutterstock.com (Denis and Yulia Pogostins).

Contents

Maths on the farm. 4

Counting 6

Measuring 10

Shapes 14

Time .18

Answers 22

Picture glossary 23

Index .24

Maths on the farm

Plants grow on a farm.

Animals live on a farm.

A farmer works on a farm.

A farmer uses maths.

Counting

The farmer counts seeds.

The farmer counts eggs.

The farmer counts animals.

How many cows can you count?

(answer on page 22)

Measuring

scales

The farmer measures how heavy
the fruit is.

crop

The farmer measures how much crop will be needed.

The farmer measures how long
the vegetable is.

Which horse is taller?

(answer on page 22)

Shapes

There are shapes on the land.

There are shapes in the water.

This hay makes a rectangle.

What shape does this hay make?

(answer on page 22)

Time

The farmer knows what time to water the plants.

The farmer knows what time
to feed the animals.

The farmer plants seeds in
the spring.

The farmer harvests the plants.

What season is this?

(answer on page 22)

21

Answers

page 9: There are three cows.

page 13: The dark horse is taller than the light brown horse.

page 17: The hay makes circles.

page 21: The season is autumn.

Picture glossary

harvest to pick and gather plants when they are ready

seed small plant part that can grow into a new plant

Index

cows 9
eggs 7
hay 16, 17
horse 13
seasons 20, 21

Notes for parents and teachers
Maths is a way that we make sense of the world around us. For the young child, this includes recognizing similarities and differences, classifying objects, recognizing shapes and patterns, developing number sense, and using simple measurement skills.

Before reading
Connect with what children know
Ask children to name some things they have recently eaten, and discuss how those items, and most of our food, came from a farm. Talk about the work that people do on farms, working with plants and animals. Encourage children to discuss any experience they have had visiting a farm or learning about the plants and animals that grow on farms.

After reading
Build upon children's curiosity and desire to explore
- Revisit the picture on page 7 of a farmer counting eggs. Ask children if they know how we usually buy eggs in a shop (in a box of 6 or 12 eggs). Explain that a dozen is another name for 12. Have an empty egg box available and allow children to practise counting 12 objects into the spaces of the box.
- Discuss how time and seasons are very important to the job of the farmer. Review the four seasons and talk about how plants and animals grow around the seasons. Collect photos that show farms across the seasons and ask children to sort the photos by season.